D1526465

Pesticides

Necessary Risk

Charlene W. Billings

— Issues in Focus —

ENSLOW PUBLISHERS, INC.

Bloy St. & Ramsey Ave.	P.O. Box 38
Box 777	Aldershot
Hillside, N.J. 07205	Hants GU12 6BP
U.S.A.	U.K.

PARLIN MEMORIAL LIBRARY
EVERETT, MASS.

363.1792
B598p

*In memory of Rachel Carson, whose warning about the
dangers of the indiscriminate use of pesticides, published
in 1962 in* Silent Spring, *puts all people in her debt.*

Copyright © 1993 by Charlene W. Billings

All rights reserved.

No part of this book may be reprinted by any means
without the written permission of the publisher.

Library of Congress Cataloging-In-Publication Data

Billings, Charlene W.
     Pesticides : necessary risk / Charlene W. Billings
        p. cm. — (Issues in focus)
     Includes bibliographical references and index.
     Summary: Examines the history and uses of pesticides, their
advantages and disadvantages, their regulation, and the idea that
they are a necessary risk in order to feed the world.
     ISBN 0-89490-299-7
     1. Pesticides—Juvenile literature. 2. Pesticides—Environmental
aspects—Juvenile literature. 3. Pesticide residues in food—
Juvenile literature. 4. Pesticides—Government policy—United
States—Juvenile literature. [1.Pesticides.] I. Title.
II. Series: Issues in focus (Hillside, N.J.)
SB951.13.B55   1993
363.17'92—dc20   92-30394
                                       CIP
                                       AC
Printed in the U.S.A.

10 9 8 7 6 5 4 3 2 1

Illustration Credits:
© Erich Hartmann, 1961, Used by permission of the Rachel Carson
Council, Inc., p. 22; International Apple Institute, p. 95; Tanimura & Antle
Photo, p. 101; Tea Council of the U.S.A., Inc., p. 65; U.S. Department of
Agriculture, pp. 10, 13, 14, 60, 76, 79, 84; USDA/Tim McCabe, p. 41;
USDA/Buford J. Poe, p. 69; USDA/Doug Wilson, pp. 32, 39; U.S. Food
and Drug Administration, pp. 6, 56; United Nations Photo, pp. 17, 20, 27,
36; U.S. Fish and Wildlife Service, Luther Goldman. p. 43; Washington
Apple Commission, pp. 49, 52.

Cover Photo:
© Peter J. Bryant/Biological Photo Service

Contents

Acknowledgements

My sincere appreciation to everyone who has shared their knowledge about pesticides with me and provided information and photographs for this book. Special thanks to Dr. David Pimentel of Cornell University and Mr. Lindsay Moose of the U.S. Environmental Protection Agency who read the manuscript for accuracy. Their expert, helpful suggestions have assisted greatly in the preparation of the manuscript for this book.

In addition, I wish to thank Dr. Alan T. Eaton, Extension Specialist, Pest Management, Cooperative Extension Service, University of New Hampshire, Durham, New Hampshire, for sharing his experience and information about integrated pest management.

Thank you to Margaret J. Pratt, Agriculture Extension Educator, Hillsborough County Extension, Milford, New Hampshire, for welcoming me to use the many books and other valuable resource materials available at her office.

My appreciation also to Catherine A. Violette, M.S., R.D., Extension Specialist, Food and Nutrition, University of New Hampshire, Durham, New Hampshire, for providing videos and other sources of information about pesticides and foods for use in this book.

Preface

The safety of our food supply and the well-being of the environment are public concerns that are important to each of us. Parents want to be assured that the foods they offer to their children are truly safe to eat. They also desire to pass on to their children a clean world that is environmentally sound and capable of sustaining and enriching the lives of future generations. These goals are common to all human beings.

In writing this book I sought to present some of the questions about safety in the use of pesticides, the origins of synthetic pesticides, where residues are found, and how pesticides are regulated. In some of the examples mentioned, I have presented opposing points of view about the use of pesticides so that the reader can reach a better understanding of the complexity of the problems.

Studies have shown that with proper management, the quantity of synthetic pesticides used on some major crops can be decreased significantly without reducing crop yields. One thing is certain, each of us has a stake in ensuring a safe, adequate food supply and a clean environment for the future benefit of all people.

Charlene W. Billings

Many of the food products pictured here would not be as abundant or as inexpensive if pesticides were not used. However, public concern about safety of many foods has led to a reexamination of the proper use of pesticides.

1

The Constant Pests

According to a survey by the World Future Society, people fear damage to the earth's environment and natural resources more than they fear nuclear war or an arms race. This fear is not surprising when you consider that the survival of all forms of life, including our own, depends upon the earth's natural resources.

One area of concern for many people is the protection of ourselves and our environment from the unwise use of pesticides. A pest is a plant, animal, or organism that is harmful to health, property, crops, or the environment. And a pesticide is a substance that kills or lessens the effects of pests.

There are many examples of the unwise use of pesticides.

A brief account of one such history points out the need for our concern:

> In the Great Lakes region of the United States, fishing is an important multimillion dollar business as well as a greatly loved sport. During the first half of the 1900s, many of the fish that lived in the Great Lakes, such as trout, salmon, and blue pike, significantly declined in numbers. Where once there were many, now there were few. One reason was that the Great Lakes were overfished, but another was that the fish were being preyed upon by sea lampreys.
>
> Millions of dollars were spent on joint programs to save the fishing industry by the Great Lakes Fishery Commission, the Department of the Interior, the Fish and Wildlife Service, and other affected parties. The purpose of these programs was to curb overfishing, to control the sea lamprey, and to restock fish in the Great Lakes. Success appeared in sight when a serious new problem surfaced.
>
> In 1964 the National Pesticide Monitoring Program was started by the United States Department of Agriculture (USDA). When the Fish and Wildlife Service monitored newly stocked salmon from the Great Lakes, it found that the fish were contaminated with high levels of two pesticides—DDT (dichloro-diphenyl-trichloro-ethane) and dieldrin. The state of Michigan recalled salmon that already had been shipped to market and embargoed it. None could be sold.
>
> The culprit pesticides had been sprayed extensively in Michigan to try to control two pests,

Dutch elm disease and Japanese beetles. Because these pesticides had found their way into the waters of the Great Lakes, salmon and other fish from these waters were too tainted to eat. The salmon fishing industry was brought to a halt for over ten years in Michigan before the fish once again were safe to eat.

When pesticides first began to be used widely, they appeared to be the answer to the age-old problem of controlling the countless kinds of constant pests that have destroyed vital crops and plagued people throughout history. And the dangers from their indiscriminate use were not yet commonly known.

Farmers know the many kinds of agricultural pests. The major animal pests include insects, mites, eelworms, rats, and mice. Examples of plant pests are weeds, bacteria, viruses, and fungal diseases such as blights, rusts, and smuts. The devastating effects of fungal, bacterial, and viral diseases on crops, livestock, and people point out the importance of being able to control them.

Animal Pests

Insects. Of the estimated three million species of insects on Earth, about 10,000 are pests. Some of these are major destroyers of crops that people grow for food for themselves or livestock. Insects are placed into two groups that have different ways of reproducing.

When a member of one group of insects reproduces, its eggs hatch into miniature insects that look just like

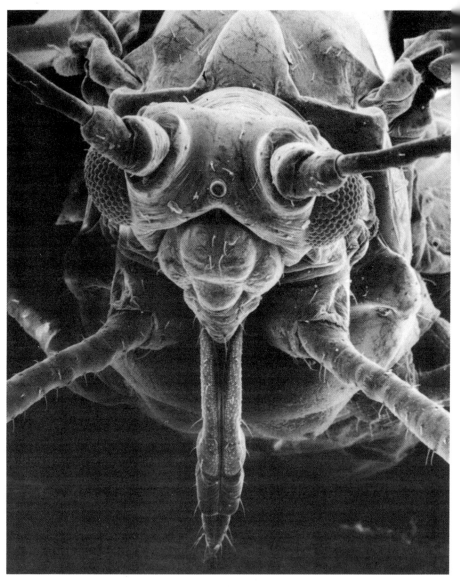

The aphid shown in this electron micrograph is nearly 200 times life size. Aphids and other insects cause major damage to crops each year by sucking the juices out of plants or eating them.

the parents. Locusts and crickets are examples of the members of this group. Swarms of locusts and crickets can consume enormous areas of valuable vegetation and crops.

The egg of an insect belonging to the second group hatches into a wormlike creature or caterpillar known as a larva. The larva of an insect in this group usually eats plants voraciously until it enters a resting stage of its life called the pupa. Later an insect that looks like the parents emerges from the pupa. Flies, such as the common housefly, and moths, such as the corn borer and codling moth, are members of this group. Generally, insects that undergo this change during their life cycles are the most destructive to crops.

Mites. Mites are related to spiders and include many animal and plant pests. For example, the citrus rust mite is a serious pest of citrus fruit crops. Ticks, which are the largest mites, are carriers of many diseases, such as Lyme disease, Rocky Mountain spotted fever, tularemia, Texas fever, and relapsing fever, to mention only a few examples.

Eelworms. Eelworms belong to the group of worms known as roundworms. Although eelworms are only about a millimeter in length, they can cause havoc when they infest crops. Affected plants become stunted and wilt in the fields. An example is the potato cyst eelworm, which has caused major crop losses in every country where potatoes are grown.

Plant Pests

Fungal Diseases. Some fungal diseases can devastate crops. The ones of greatest concern to farmers are blights, rusts, and smuts.

In Ireland in 1845, potato blight was so severe that it wiped out nearly the entire potato crop. Because potatoes were the staple crop for the country, over a million Irish people died of starvation and another million immigrated to the United States to survive.

Fire blight is a common disease of pear, apple, and other fruit trees. This disease kills cells in fruit trees so quickly that portions of the tree appear to have been burned by fire.

Rust and smuts are fungal diseases that attack a variety of agricultural crops. Wheat rust is an example of a fungal disease with a complicated life cycle. It requires two plants to survive: wheat and barberry bushes. The loss of wheat can be reduced by the elimination of barberry bushes in wheat-growing areas. However, a single undiscovered barberry bush can produce enough wheat rust fungus to infect hundreds of acres of wheat.

One smut disease, known as ergot, attacks grains and replaces the seeds forming on the plant with hard, black tissue. If people eat grain that has been infected, they suffer hallucinations. In the Middle Ages, the effect on humans was called St. Anthony's Fire because people

Rusts and smuts are fungal diseases that attack a wide range of crops. Pictured here is stem rust on wheat plants.

Helicopter spraying insecticide onto lettuce and cauliflower in Salinas, California. A study done by scientists at Cornell University showed that only one-half or less of pesticide applied by aircraft actually reaches the targeted crop.

imagined that they were on fire after eating flour made with the smut-infected grain.

Bacteria. Although many bacteria are beneficial, some are serious pests that affect crops and people. Bacteria cause soft rot in many kinds of vegetables both in the field and in storage. Cabbage infected with black rot wilts before it can be harvested.

Viruses. Viruses are so small that they cannot be seen with a microscope. For convenience they are placed with the plant pests here, but usually they are classified as neither plants nor animals. Viruses cause many important diseases of plants, animals, and people.

Weeds. Weeds are plants that grow where they are not wanted, often crowding out or using up nutrients that are needed by agricultural crops. Weeds also compete with crops for water and light. Some weeds entwine themselves around crop plants, choking their growth, and many weeds are homes for pests such as insects or fungi. Some weeds are poisonous to grazing stock animals. In addition, seeds from weeds may taint harvested food crops—wild onion plants may give a flavor to flour that makes it worthless.

Since the dawn of agriculture, farmers have been in a constant contest with an array of threatening pests that destroy crops and livestock. This struggle has led them to seek ways to combat the pests that devastate food supplies.

2

Synthetic Chemical Pest Control

For most of humanity, the greatest continuing struggle is to raise and store enough food for survival. In many areas of the world, food is not plentiful enough much of the time. And in the event of a drought or infestation with a crop-destroying pest, people go hungry. It is no wonder that at the time of their discovery, synthetic pesticides were cause for new optimism by farmers all over the world.

The effort to produce enough food for human survival has led to the constant search for better ways to prevent pests from destroying food crops and livestock. When it was discovered that certain chemicals were effective in getting rid of pests such as insects, fungal diseases, and weeds, farmers were eager to use them.

A chemical—natural or synthetic—that kills living

Many people in many countries throughout the world do not get enough to eat. These children can count on one solid meal each day through a United Nations program.

things is a biocide. A biocide poisons pests such as harmful insects, but it also may kill other harmless or helpful living things. Among the biocides are the pesticides or chemicals that are used to kill pests.

Pesticides are placed into four specific categories as well. A pesticide that kills insects is called an insecticide. In addition, a chemical that kills fungi is a fungicide, and a chemical that kills weeds is an herbicide. A rodenticide kills rodents such as rats and mice.

Insecticides and the Story of DDT

Since they became available, insecticides have been used widely throughout the world to control insect pests. One group of these insecticides is known as chlorinated hydrocarbons and includes DDT, dieldrin, chlordane, and heptachlor. The most famous of these is the white powder known as DDT (DDT is a shortened name for the chemical dichloro-diphenyl-trichloroethane).

DDT was first made in the laboratory by a German chemist, Othmar Zeidler, in 1874. However DDT's effectiveness as an insecticide was not discovered until 1939 when Paul Muller, a Swiss chemist who later won the Nobel Prize for his work, synthesized and tested it. During World War II, DDT was used to treat soldiers' uniforms to kill insect pests and disease carriers, such as body lice that could transmit deadly typhus. Indeed, DDT was cheap and easy to manufacture, so it became the most widely used insecticide.

18

One of the features of the chlorinated hydrocarbons is that they are very stable. They do not break down into harmless chemicals in the environment but instead persist for many years after being applied to control pests. Because of this stability, DDT and the other chemicals in this group sometimes are called "hard" pesticides.

All of the chlorinated hydrocarbons are synthetic, or manufactured in laboratories. They were not present in nature before their use to control pests began during World War II. These chemicals act as nerve poisons and kill pests by interfering with normal nerve function.

At first DDT was celebrated as a godsend for humankind. Spectacularly, it prevented a typhus epidemic in Naples, Italy, in 1944, where it was dusted onto 1,300,000 civilians. In addition, it halted an epidemic of plague in Dakar, Africa.

But as time passed, doubts arose. Some scientists were concerned that DDT and other related insecticides would have serious long-term effects on the environment. And in the 1950s evidence began to appear that these stable chemicals not only persisted in the environment, they accumulated in the fatty tissues of animals.

In 1958 a warning was published by Roy Barker of the Illinois Natural History Survey at Urbana. The survey told how DDT sprayed on elm trees to control Dutch elm disease was found in earthworms that burrowed in and ate the fallen elm leaves. Countless robins died when they ate the DDT-tainted earthworms. The

Locusts invade North Africa in November of 1954, in what used to be known as French Morocco. The people in this picture are feeding poison bait to the locusts in a United Nations Food and Agriculture Organization (FAO) program to fight the invasion. Vast swarms of locusts strip all vegetation as they migrate through an area.

leaves of the elm tree, the earthworms feeding beneath the elm tree, and the robins that ate the earthworms were the links of a tainted food chain through which DDT passed.

Another important problem with DDT was detected as early as 1947 in Sweden. DDT had been used liberally in that country against houseflies. But soon it was found that the houseflies were not being killed as readily by DDT as they once had been. The flies had become resistant to the insecticide.

Scientists reasoned that populations of flies usually contain a few individuals that are not affected by DDT. These resistant flies survive, reproduce, and eventually give rise to a largely resistant population of flies. The same phenomenon began to be seen in other countries where disease-carrying mosquitoes and pests of cotton became resistant to DDT.

Rachel Carson and Silent Spring. Another person who issued a warning against the indiscriminate use of pesticides such as DDT was Rachel Carson. She sounded an alarm in her landmark book *Silent Spring* published in 1962. The book was described by Justice William O. Douglas as ". . . the most important chronicle of this century for the human race."

Silent Spring gained worldwide fame and made the public aware of environmental problems. The book and the public pressure prompted by it led government officials to take action to protect the environment against

Rachel Carson warned the world of the dangers of DDT in her book *Silent Spring*. As a result of her warning, the public became aware of the environmental problems DDT created, which led to its banning in the United States, Canada, and many other countries of the world.

persistant pesticides, as well as other forms of water, air, and soil pollution.

Banning DDT. DDT was almost totally banned by the Environmental Protection Agency (EPA) in the United States by the end of 1972. Many other countries, including Canada, Sweden, and Denmark, had already banned the pesticide.

Despite the drawbacks of DDT, some experts do not agree with a total ban on its use. In an article in the *Wall Street Journal* on September 12, 1989, Kenneth Mellanby, a British entomologist who has studied pesticides for fifty years, presents a different point of view. He argues that DDT has a great advantage of being relatively nontoxic to humans. No one has ever died from using it as an insecticide. (In the same article Mellanby states, "The only fatal poisoning reported was when it was mistaken for flour and used, neat, in pancakes.") He believes that DDT was totally banned from use in many countries prematurely.

Some Third World countries still use DDT for indoor spraying against mosquitoes that carry malaria. This usage contributes little to the pollution of the outside environment. In contrast, in Third World countries such as India where DDT has been banned, malaria has recurred in epidemic proportions. In 1961, India had 40,000 cases of malaria. Today the number of cases has exploded to 60,000,000.

Organic Phosphates. Another major group of insecticides is known as organic phosphates. This group includes parathion and malathion, among other chemicals. These newer chemical pesticides are less persistent in the environment that the chlorinated hydrocarbons. However, they are much more toxic to both man and animals.

In her book *Silent Spring*, Rachel Carson describes the poisoning of people who apply organic phosphates or who accidentally come into contact with drifting spray, a discarded container, or plants that have been treated. Two children in Florida found an empty bag that had contained parathion. They used the bag to repair a swing. Within a short time, both of the children died. In Wisconsin, another child died when the parathion spray his father was applying to potatoes drifted from the nearby field to where he was playing.

In California, eleven of thirty men became extremely ill after picking oranges that had been sprayed with parathion two and one-half weeks earlier. And residues of parathion have been detected in orange peels six months after the oranges were sprayed with this pesticide.

Among many other uses, malathion is sprayed from low-flying helicopters to eradicate the Mediterranean fruit fly from California orange groves. Beginning in early January 1990, the California Food and Agriculture Department treated twenty-eight communities in Los Angeles and Orange counties. And eight to twelve sprayings were planned over the span of the following five months despite strong public protest.

Malathion has also been used to protect alfalfa

against the alfalfa weevil and cattle against horn flies. Unchecked, as many as 4,000 bloodsucking horn flies can infest one cow. Malathion used in a spray or dip can control the horn fly.

Insecticide Usage. Of the over 136 million pounds of insecticides used in the United States annually, about 25 percent is used on only two crops: corn and cotton. Usage also varies from one region of the country to another. For example, in Southern Plains states, up to 89 percent of alfalfa is treated with insecticides, but the overall alfalfa acreage treated in the United States is only 13 percent. In the Southeast and Delta states, more than twice the cotton cropland has insecticides applied to it than in the Southern Plains region.

Fungicides

In addition to insects, farmers must do battle with many different fungi that attack crops. The major applications of fungicides are on fruits and vegetables. One of the oldest fungicides is sulphur. Combined with lime, it is very effective against fungal diseases of fruit trees.

In the early 1880s, Professor P. M. A. Millardet, a botanist at the University of Bordeaux in France, noticed that some roadside grape vines still had their leaves at the end of the growing season. By October all of the other vines had been defoliated by downy mildew. He learned that the vineyard owners had sprinkled the roadside vines with copper sulphates and lime to discourage pilfering.

Professor Millardet tested the mixture to see if it would prevent mildew. When he found that it did, he published his results in 1885. The powder became known as Bordeaux mixture. The mixture later was found to be effective against potato blight as well. Bordeaux mixture became a standard fungicide and is still used today.

A group of chemicals called dicarboximides came into use as fungicides in the years following World War II. These chemicals have been used to protect the leaves and seeds of a variety of fruits such as apples, cherries, grapes, peaches, strawberries, and watermelons. They also curb powdery mildews and blights on potatoes.

Another group of fungicides, EBDCs (ethylenebis-dithiocarbamates) has been in use in the United States sinced the mid-1940s to control fungal diseases. The Environmental Protection Agency (EPA) has been reviewing the EBDCs because a breakdown product known as ETU (ethylenethiourea) has been found to cause cancer of the liver and thyroid in laboratory animals.

Though other fungicides have been developed, EBDCs have continued to be widely used because they work against a broad range of fungal diseases and are relatively inexpensive. The principal crops on which EBDCs are used are cabbage, spinach, apples, tomatoes, potatoes, and melons.

Children of the village of Gatazo Grande, Ecuador lining up to have their hair and clothing sprayed with DDT powder in this 1957 photograph. Despite the environmental hazards caused by DDT, no one has ever died from using it as an insecticide.

Herbicides

Herbicides are chemicals that are used to kill weeds. Again, there are many such chemicals in use today. Examples are alachlor to control annual grasses and some broadleaf weeds in corn and potatoes; linuron to combat weeds in asparagus, carrots, celery, onions, potatoes, parsnips, and corn; and terbacil to defeat weeds in alfalfa, apples, peaches, asparagus, blueberries, and strawberries.

The importance of herbicides in agriculture for weed control is evident from the quantities of herbicides used in the United States compared to insecticides or fungicides. In 1988 approximately 500 million pounds of herbicides were used compared to only about 136 million pounds of insecticides or about thirty million pounds of fungicides.

Another interesting fact is that nearly 75 percent of the herbicides used in the United States are applied to only two major crops: soybeans and corn. Over half of the herbicides used are applied to corn.

Rodenticides

A rodenticide is a substance used to kill mice, rats, and other rodent pests. Among the most commonly used rodenticides are warfarin (derived from the name of the foundation that patented it, Wisconsin Alumni Research

Foundation, plus coumarin), 1080 (sodium fluoroacetate), ANTU (alpha-naphthylthiourea), and red squill.

All of these chemicals prevent normal blood clotting and kill by causing internal hemorrhaging. Rodents are poisoned when they eat bait laced with one of these substances. These rodenticides are poisonous to other animals as well as rodents. However, red squill, which is obtained from the bulbs of a subtropical plant, may be less toxic to other animals because they can remove it from their stomachs by vomiting whereas rodents cannot vomit.

The control of rodents, especially rats and mice, is vitally important. Rats and mice help spread many diseases that claim human lives, including deadly typhus and plague.

In addition, every year throughout the world rats and mice destroy a significant portion of the harvested crops that are needed for food for people as well as for livestock. It is estimated that a single rat eats about forty pounds of feed each year and that it contaminates at least twice that amount.

In countries where food supplies already may be scarce, the loss of even a small percentage of a harvested crop to insect pests, fungal diseases, weeds, or rodent pilferers can be critical to the health, well-being, and lives of the people.

3

A Hungry World

As the world population continues to grow, there will be a need to increase world food production. The population of the world in 1964, for example, was estimated to be 3.2 billion people, having increased from less than one billion in the year 1800. Some projections are that the world population will grow to over nine billion by the year 2025. That is a tripling of the number of people who must be fed within a span of only sixty-one years.

North America: A Breadbasket for the World

In contrast to many other areas of the world between 1940 and 1964, food production in the United States more than kept pace with a population that increased over 47 percent. During this period, the quantity of corn grown climbed by over 61 percent, wheat grown by over 59 percent, and meat produced by over 60 percent.

There are many reasons for this extraordinary agricultural achievement. Since the early 1940s, American farms have used more and more machines, such as combined harvester-threshers and automated mechanical pickers for corn and other crops. During this time, chemical fertilizers also have contributed to the increase in crop output. The calcium, phosphorus, potassium, and nitrogen that growing plants remove from the soil were restored for future crops.

In addition, the use of pesticides to protect crops jumped from less than 100 million pounds per year in 1942 to over 560 million pounds in 1972. And by 1990 farmers applied over 700 million pounds of pesticides.

North America has become an important breadbasket for the world. Since 1950 North American exports of grain have increased over five times, from about twenty-three million tons to over 119 million tons. The increasing demand from foreign countries for our grain has resulted in more and more acreage being brought under cultivation.

The Changing Pattern of World Food Trade

There has been a change in the pattern of world food trade as well. In 1950 the bulk of the international trade in grain flowed from North America to western Europe.

Harvesting wheat in Pullman, Washington in 1983. The use of fertilizers and pesticides, combined with the use of modern techniques and machinery, such as this combined harvester, have allowed American farmers to increase the harvest from each acre of land under cultivation.

The rest of the world was pretty much self-sufficient. But there has been a dramatic shift in the last few decades, and grains increasingly are being exported now to many non-European countries.

The major U.S. export crops are corn, soybeans, and wheat. The major export fiber crop is cotton. In 1985 U.S. farmers provided more than 80 percent of the soybeans sold on the world market and more than 70 percent of the corn. It is these crops on which three-quarters of the herbicides used in the United States are applied.

In the early 1970s the Soviet Union purchased huge quantities of U.S. grain. In 1979 the Soviet Union bought more U.S. wheat than was grown in Texas and South Dakota combined. In 1981 the People's Republic of China purchased as much wheat as could have been grown in the entire states of Nebraska and Montana, 280 million bushels. In December 1990, the Soviet Union again asked the United States and other countries for food assistance because of shortages brought about by the political upheaval in that country.

According to the United Nations Food and Agriculture Organization and the United States Department of Agriculture's Foreign Agricultural Service, Africa has had a record population increase and at the same time has suffered environmental deterioration. Egypt, Libya, Tunisia, Morocco, and Algeria now import half of the grain they consume. Even with imports of approximately twenty-eight million tons of grain in 1988, millions of sub-Saharan people did not have enough to eat, and some were on the edge of starvation.

Latin America could not produce enough grain to be self-sufficient during the 1970s, and the continent has become a grain-deficit region. In 1988 the region imported about eleven million tons of grain.

The region that leads in food importing is Asia. The amount of cropland per person in Asia has steadily been shrinking. Asia's imports of grain have risen from six million metric tons in 1950 to about eighty-nine million metric tons in 1988, a nearly fifteen-fold increase in less than forty years. This trend is expected to continue in the 1990s and into the next century.

Reduction in the World Food Supply

Of greatest concern is the decline in world grain stocks, which have been reduced significantly in recent years. In 1987 the amount of grain in storage worldwide was at a record level of 459 million tons. This is enough grain to feed the world for about one hundred days. By 1989 this reserve of food was down to enough to feed the world for only about sixty days, the lowest level since the mid-1970s.

This precipitous situation has come about because as the world population has increased, worldwide grain production has dropped at a record rate. In 1987 alone, grain crops in India were reduced by eighty-five million tons due to severe monsoons. And in 1988 the most severe drought on record dramatically cut grain production in the United States. For the first time ever, the United States' grain harvest was below the country's consumption rate.

The only way the United States could supply exports to other countries during 1988 and 1989 was to sell its stockpiled grain from previous harvests. More than one year of severe drought in a row could lead to a world food crisis.

The World Bank defines food insecure people as those who do not have enough food for normal health and physical activity. In Ethiopia alone it is estimated that 14.7 million people, or about one-third of the population, are undernourished (food insecure). Nigeria has 13.7 million who do not get enough to eat. And in the countries of Chad, Mozambique, Uganda, and Somalia, at least 40 percent of the people are chronically food insecure. A recently published article by Werner Fornos, president of the Population Institute, estimates that almost one-third of the population of Africa, nearly 200 million people, is hungry and malnourished.

United Nations World Food Council Report. In 1988, in the United Nations World Food Council's report "The Global State of Hunger and Malnutrition," the council pointed out that Africa is not alone in its battle to avert hunger. In Latin America as well, per capita grain production has fallen 7 percent since 1981. The number of malnourished preschoolers in Peru increased from 42 percent to 68 percent in the years 1980 to 1983 alone. And infant deaths, which are

In Ethiopia, the World Bank estimates that there are over fourteen million people who are food insecure. The children in this picture are being served milk as part of a relief program.

viewed as an indicator of nutritional well-being, have increased in Brazil during the decade of the 1980s.

The council's summary of its report states that "earlier progress in fighting hunger, malnutrition, and poverty has come to a halt or is being reversed in many parts of the world."

Although pesticides may pose some risks, these dangers must be weighed against the need to combat serious pests such as harmful insects, fungal diseases, bacteria, and viruses that destroy food supplies vital to human life and well-being.

Expansion of the Export Harvest

According to Resources for the Future, the demand for U.S. agricultural products will continue to grow. This organization projects that U.S. grain exports will rise at least 24 percent between the years 1985 and 2000. Smaller increases also are predicted for exports of meat, milk, and oilseed crops. In addition, by the year 2000, the United States Census Bureau estimates that farmers will need to feed over 300 million Americans alone.

In response to the demand, farmers in the United States have expanded their wheat production since the first Soviet grain purchases. The area harvested grew from forty-four million acres in 1970 to seventy-eight million acres in 1982, nearly doubling within twelve years. Although the Great Plains area of the United States is the traditional wheat-growing region, much of the expansion was in the Corn Belt and the South. This was accomplished by "double cropping."

Double cropping used new herbicides and planting machinery that eliminated plowing and other field work. A crop of winter wheat was planted after the fall harvest of soybeans. The following June, the wheat could be harvested and soybeans planted directly into the wheat stubble remaining in the fields. Using these techniques along with improved plant varieties, U.S. wheat production increased by 30 percent from 1976 to 1982.

In addition to wheat, the U.S. production of other major export crops has increased steadily as well. Farmers in the United States have increased both the number of plantings and their yields per acre. The result has been that during the early 1980s they raised almost twice as much corn and soybeans per year as they did in 1970.

As U.S. farmers have brought more land into production for export crops, concern has grown for the effect on our natural resources and environment. For example, pasture and hay fields in the Corn Belt, as well as rangeland in the West have been plowed and planted with crops. In addition, wetlands in the lower Mississippi River Valley have been drained to plant soybeans. This has resulted in increased soil erosion and pollution of water resources with agricultural chemicals.

American farmers nearly doubled the number of acres of farmland devoted to wheat production during twelve years starting in 1970. The area harvested grew from forty-four million acres in 1970 to seventy-eight million acres in 1982.

4

Pesticide Residues in Groundwater

Since the founding of our country, American farmers have been looked upon as stewards of the environment. However, since the 1970s, a time when U.S. grain exports began to rise sharply, the public has become more aware that some agricultural practices contribute to soil erosion, loss of productive farm land, and contamination of surface and subsurface water.

Agricultural Runoff

Soil erosion from farms causes damage to the environment by loss of valuable topsoil. But in addition, soil erosion pollutes air and water with residues of fertilizers and pesticides. Croplands most affected by erosion are those used for corn, soybeans, and cotton. In 1977, one-third of the land planted with corn lost five tons of

Agricultural runoff is shown in this picture of the erosion of fine soils from an unprotected corn field on a western Tennessee farm after a brief storm in 1982. Fertilizers and pesticides contained in agricultural runoff end up in streams, lakes, and drinking water.

topsoil per acre for the year. Similar losses were recorded for land planted with cotton and even greater losses for land planted with soybeans.

Eroded soil and water runoff from farmlands, with their burden of chemical fertilizers and pesticides, are broadly dispersed into our water supplies. Cities have been able to clean up localized sources of water pollution such as industrial and sewage discharges, but erosion and water runoff from farms have been a more difficult water quality problem to pinpoint and solve.

The EPA's Office of Water Planning and Standards estimated that 2.1 million fish were killed in 1980 as a result of pesticide, fertilizer, or other farm-related runoff in the water. In 1976 a pesticide runoff killed over 100,000 fish in an Alabama fish hatchery. In Louisiana the herbicide paraquat has killed crayfish and shrimp.

When the quantities of pesticides used for agriculture are compared to other uses, over 73 percent of all pesticides used are applied to farm acreage. Government and industrial lands use over 12 percent and household lands a similar amount. In addition, a small percentage of the total quantity of pesticides used in the United States is on forest lands.

Contamination of Groundwater

Water that saturates cracks and porous rock formations beneath the surface of the Earth is known as groundwater. Groundwater is vitally important because it is the

More than one type of pollution can be seen in this photo of an Alaskan pond. In areas where pesticides have been found in surface and groundwater, more than one type can usually be detected.

principal underlying source of springwater and wellwater used by people.

Evidence of pesticide runoff from seventeen agricultural chemicals contaminating groundwater has been found in at least twenty-three states. However, the Council of Environmental Quality, a governmental advisory organization, estimated in 1984 that only about 2 percent of all groundwater is contaminated. Most of this contaminated water is near high population centers and does not result from farming practices.

Nevertheless, a 1984 Iowa Geological Survey study found pesticides such as Sencor (metrabuzin), Lasso (alachlor), Bladex (cyanazine), and Dual (metolachlor) in two out of every three wells tested that were located in the northeastern part of the state. Some of these regions have bedrock riddled with fissures and natural porosity that allow runoff to rapidly enter the groundwater. These formations are located in over 6,000 square miles of Iowa.

During the Iowa study, evidence was found that some pesticides once believed to decompose quickly in the environment persist in the groundwater. Some of these pesticides are thought to be carcinogenic. Alachlor may cause cancers of the lungs, thyroid, and stomach in laboratory animals.

More recently, when Iowa's natural resources department and the University of Iowa tested the quality of groundwater in 686 rural wells in 1988 and 1989, they found that nearly 15 percent were contaminated with one or more pesticides.

State officials in Florida have detected groundwater contamination from agricultural pesticides such as ethylene dibromide (EDB), which has been used widely to control rootworm in the Florida citrus fruit growing regions. Florida uses groundwater almost exclusively for its drinking water supplies, so these findings also raise serious concerns.

Groundwater Protection

Several federal laws are designed to protect groundwater. Among them are the Clean Water Act (1977) and the Safe Drinking Water Act (1974 and 1980). The Clean Water Act (CWA) gives the EPA authority over the quality of surface and groundwater. One of the provisions of Section 208 of the CWA focuses on nonpoint sources of pollution, which includes agricultural and urban runoff.

The Environmental Protection Agency (EPA) has legally enforceable standards for traces of pesticides in public drinking water. These standards are spelled out in the Safe Drinking Water Act. The EPA uses maximum contaminant levels (MCLs) and health advisories (HAs) to guide public health officials and others who may encounter problems with water contamination. The MCLs and HAs are values that represent the maximum groundwater residue levels that are considered safe by the EPA.

The values assume that a person consumes about one-half gallon of water daily over his or her entire lifetime and include a 100 to 1,000 percent margin of safety.

For example, the MCL for the pesticide alachlor is two parts per billion, an extremely dilute solution. If the pesticide were measured in ounces, then one ounce of alachlor would be dissolved in a billion ounces or 7,800,000 gallons of water. To put this in perspective, if an aspirin tablet were cut into six equal pieces and one of the pieces was dissolved in 16,000 gallons of water (the approximate volume of a railroad tank car), there would be about one part per billion aspirin in the water solution. If you drank one-half gallon of water from the tank car each day, it would take eighty-eight years to drink all the 16,000 gallons and swallow the one-sixth aspirin tablet.

Pesticide Residues
in Food

In addition to pesticides in groundwater, consumers are concerned about pesticide residues on or in foods they buy. An article in the October 1988 issue of *FDA Consumer* states that recent surveys have shown that pesticide residues are the public's number one food safety fear. Do pesticide residues present a serious human health hazard?

The Alar-on-Apples Scare

Alar is a chemical sprayed on some red apples, primarily Delicious, Staymen, and McIntosh. It is used to regulate their growth, to keep them on the tree longer to ripen, and to let them turn red naturally. This chemical, also known as daminozide, had been used since the 1960s by apple growers. Alar gained wide publicity recently because tests in laboratory animals indicated the chemical may be a carcinogen (cancer-causing agent).

Alar sprayed onto apples cannot be removed by washing or peeling. In addition, Alar forms UDMH (unsymmetrical dimethylhydrazine) when it is heated during the processing of apples into applesauce or apple juice. According to the EPA, UDMH may be a potent animal carcinogen.

Much of the concern about Alar is due to the fact that children consume many more apples as processed apple products than adults do. A preschool child may drink up to eighteen times more apple juice than his or her parent. In addition, laboratory studies have indicated that young animals are more susceptible to a given dose of a carcinogen than older animals.

Dr. William Lijinski was the head of a research laboratory at the National Cancer Institute when he was asked how serious the risk of Alar is by the CBS-TV news show *60 Minutes* in February 1989. He answered:

> I don't think it's as serious as some reports have made out that it is. It is—there's no question that Alar either is a carcinogen or it produces a carcinogen, unsymmetrical dimethyl hydrazine. Nobody is going to get cancer from exposure to Alar in apples alone, but it is going to increase their cancer risk, and in a number of people that's going to put them over the edge and they'll develop cancer during their lifetime.

Apples being harvested before being shipped to market. Consumers have demanded perfect looking apples, which led to the Alar-on-Apples scare of 1989. Tests in laboratory animals indicated that alar may be a cancer causing agent.

The EPA estimates that from 5 to 15 percent of the United States apple crop was treated with Alar as late as the spring of 1989. When Consumers Union of the United States, Inc., publishers of the magazine *Consumer Reports,* tested thirty-two samples of apple juice from New York state markets in 1988, two out of three samples had some Alar present in them. (Samples gathered by the EPA were from more diverse locations.) And Alar also was present in samples that came from manufacturers that claimed they no longer used Alar-treated apples.

In a published letter appearing in the May 19, 1989, issue of *Science,* Edward Groth III of Consumers Union stated:

> The scientific facts (estimates of how big the risk is, with all the inherent uncertainties) are just *part* of what the public knows about Alar. The policy choices—both the personal and the public kind—depend on far more than facts.

Groth continued,

> For instance, most people probably do not know whether Alar poses a real cancer threat or not, but they know some experts think it *may.* And they prefer not to gamble with their own or their children's health. . . . Alar is present in apple products without their consent or knowledge and . . . consumers can do nothing on their own to detect or remove it.

The Natural Resources Defense Council (NRDC) published a report, *Intolerable Risk: Pesticides in Our*

Children's Food, that asserted that children were at risk from the presence of Alar and other pesticide residues on foods. However, an independent panel of scientists reading the published report found that its conclusions were based on the quantities of pesticide residues present on raw produce just after harvest, not the quantities present at the time the produce was eaten.

The average amount of Alar residue on treated apples was found to be one part per million; the EPA allows twenty parts per million. In addition, the highest level of Alar found in apple juice by Consumers Union was 1.8 parts per million. As for UDMH, the amount of residue is far less than for Alar. When Consumers Union tested apple juice, it contained only eighteen parts per billion of UDMH.

If Alar is compared to carcinogens that are in many other foods we regularly eat, it is seen to be a minimal hazard. For example, if the hazard for Alar is ranked as one, the hazard from carcinogens naturally found in foods like mushrooms, brown mustard, and peanut butter would rank as one hundred, seventy, and thirty respectively.

The accuracy of the NRDC report was clouded further when the California Department of Food and Agriculture found that the NRDC had excluded food samples with no detectable pesticide residues. This omission exaggerated the estimates of pesticide consumption up to 500 times.

Children eat a larger number of apples than adults. Authorities were afraid that Alar-treated apples could possibly cause harm to many children.

The British Advisory Committee on Pesticides studied tests done on Alar and UDMH. Their conclusion was that "even for children consuming the maximum quantities of apples and apple juice, subjected to the maximum treatment with daminozide, there is no risk."

The FDA, the USDA, and the EPA issued a joint statement that these agencies did not believe that eating apples posed a hazard to the health of children. They encouraged school systems and others to serve apples to children.

Effects of the Scare

Apples growers were adversely affected by the many reports on possible cancer risk from eating Alar-treated apples. In the spring of 1989, reports about Alar resulted in many school cafeterias banning and some supermarket chains refusing to carry fruit treated with Alar.

Some consumers turned away from buying red apples, even from growers that had not used Alar for several years. In a May 14, 1989, interview by Ed Bradley on the CBS-TV news show, *60 Minutes,* Washington apple grower Jay Sandlin said:

> If it's true that you have found that consumers want Alar-free apples, we have them, and we have millions of boxes of them that are going to be thrown away because there's no market now, Ed, after your program.

The International Apple Institute estimated that

growers lost over one hundred million dollars in the early part of 1989 due to the controversy over Alar on apples.

On June 2, 1989, Uniroyal Chemical Company, the manufacturers of Alar, announced that it was voluntarily taking Alar off the United States market immediately. The company defended the chemical as safe but stated that its continued use on apples in this country "is causing doubt and confusion about the safety of America's food supply."

Janet Hathaway, an attorney for NRDC in Washington, said:

> The Alar controversy served as a sparkplug for public concern. Now, there is activity under way to translate that concern into lasting pesticide reform. Alar was symptomatic of the problems that permeate the whole regulatory process.

Captan

Among the fruits that have been sprayed with the fungicide captan are apples, cherries, strawberries, peaches, and watermelons. In 1980 the EPA began a review of captan, which now is considered to be a carcinogen. By 1985 the EPA proposed a ban on the fungicide after reviewing animal studies and making assumptions about the amount of residue on foods.

Within weeks growers and chemical companies showed that the quantity of residue on sixty-six products on which captan was used was much lower than the EPA had estimated. In early May of 1989, the EPA banned the use of captan on forty-two crops but allowed farmers to spray it on twenty-four others. In 1990, the EPA placed more restrictions on captan use.

Dioxin

Another example of a chemical inadvertently finding its way into food is that of dioxin. Actually, there are seventy-five different compounds that are dioxins. However, the best-known and most toxic dioxin is 2,3,7,8-tetrachloro-dibenzo-p-dioxin, or TCDD.

The dioxin TCDD has been shown to cause cancer in animals and has been linked with an increase in the number of cases of certain rare cancers in humans. It also can cause a disfiguring skin disease in humans called chloracne. The EPA has called dioxin "one of the most perplexing and potentially dangerous chemicals ever to pollute the environment."

Arnold Schechter, a professor of preventive medicine at State University of New York in Binghamton, has said, "In the United States we've found that everyone's got dioxin in them." And the same findings are true of Europeans and Canadians, according to researchers. One concern that results from these data is that the statistics treated as normal cancer incidences for the general population may be due, at least in part, from our exposure to low doses of these chemicals.

Dioxin, a compound which has been linked to rare cancers in humans, was found in milk cartons in 1988. The dioxin in milk comes from chlorine-bleached paper milk cartons. Pressure from consumers has led the producers of milk cartons to reduce the dioxin levels by changing the packaging.

In 1988 dioxin was discovered in milk that had come from the chlorine-bleached paper milk cartons used for packaging. The FDA analyzed milk samples from fifteen packaging plants in the United States and found dioxin and a related compound at levels below one part per trillion (ppt).

In September 1989 the president of the American Paper Institute, Red Cavaney, told a hearing of the House Energy and Commerce health subcommittee that 75 percent of milk carton producers had reduced dioxin levels in packaging to two ppt. This is a level that cannot be distinguished from the background level of dioxin already in milk. And by the end of 1990, the dioxin levels in milk caused by paper cartons was to have been reduced by all of the milk carton industry.

Greenpeace testified at the same hearing before the House Energy and Commerce health subcommittee. They advocate the use of unbleached milk cartons.

Another dietary source of dioxin may be contaminated fish. Researchers reported in May 1985, that there were traces of dioxin in fish from some areas in the Great Lakes and elsewhere. However the presence of TCDD in fish was not widespread. Instead it appears to be localized in areas near production sites. Some less toxic dioxins have been found in eggs, bacon, chicken, pork chops, and beef liver in studies done by the FDA since 1979. Their presence appears to be related to the agricultural use of a chemical, pentachlorophenol, used as a general fungicide, bactericide, and wood preservative.

Studies done in Sweden and other Scandinavian countries suggest that another source of dietary dioxin contamination is air pollution from municipal, industrial, and hazardous-waste incinerators. A study done in Sweden found that dioxins can be formed during the burning of polyvinyl chloride and some organic chemicals and chlorinated solvents. The dioxins contaminate pastures where dairy cows graze and turn up in the milk produced by these cows. Dioxins also were measured in Baltic seals, salmon, and human breast milk.

Based on this research, Sweden's EPA enacted a moratorium on all new incinerators in February of 1985. During the moratorium, studies were done to measure the levels of dioxins in human breast milk because of its importance in infant health.

One result of the Swedish study was that incinerator operators found that they didn't have to be strong polluters. When inspected six months later, one incinerator that had been a potent source of dioxin pollution had taken measures that reduced the amount of dioxin released into the atmosphere over thirteen-fold.

EBDCs and ETU

The FDA has monitored EBDCs (ethylenebisdithiocarbamates) and ETU (ethylenethiourea) for over ten years. Between October 1, 1987, and September 6, 1989, the

FDA analyzed over 100 different foods for EBDC or ETU residues. In 90 percent of the 2,156 samples tested, no residues were detected. Only one percent had residues that exceeded the tolerances set by the EPA

In September 1989, the leading manufacturers of EBDCs asked the EPA to allow the continued use of these chemicals on thirteen crops: almonds, asparagus, corn, bananas, cranberries, grapes, figs, peanuts, potatoes, onions, sugar beets, tomatoes, and wheat.

In December 1989, the EPA proposed to cancel EBDC use on forty-five of the fifty-five crops for which EBDCs had been approved. The EPA proposal reduced the thirteen crops cited by the manufacturers to ten, eliminating from their list bananas, tomatoes, and potatoes. The Florida Fruit and Vegetable Association noted that there is no alternative fungicide that can be used to protect some crops, such as lettuce. After conducting further risk assessments on EDBCs, in March 1992, the EPA cancelled the use of EDBCs on eleven crops instead of the forty-five crops proposed at the end of 1989.

Some Pesticide Exports Boomerang

Even though chlordane was banned from agricultural use in our country in the mid-1970s, it continued to be exported to Honduras. When 80,000 pounds of Honduran beef then was imported back into the United States and distributed here, the beef was found to contain chlordane in unacceptable levels.

Beef comes from many countries besides the United States. Pesticides which are banned in the United States can still be used legally in many foreign countries. These pesticides sometimes are found in the products which are shipped to the U.S. consumers, including beef.

In addition, the Natural Resources Defense Council has found that heptachlor, which also is disallowed for agricultural use in the United States, has been used by pineapple growers in the Philippines. Later the fruit may be imported back into the United States.

The United States Food and Drug Administration (FDA) inspects food imported into the United States, but it is only able to check about one percent of all of the food sold here. In 1987 the rate of violations for imported foods, though very small, was found to be about twice that of food grown within the United States: about 5.3 percent for imported foods compared to 2.6 percent for domestic foods.

Cancer and the Delaney Clause

Special concern has been voiced about potential cancer-causing chemicals in foods. A provision of the 1958 and 1960 Food Additive Amendments, called the Delaney Clause, states that if an additive is found to cause cancer in humans or animals, it may not be added to food. And in 1968 the Delaney Clause was extended to cover residues of animal drugs in meat, eggs, and milk.

When the Delaney Clause first became law in 1958, only four known human carcinogens existed. These were radiation, tobacco smoke, beta naphthylamine (a chemical used to make dyes), and soot.

In the next three decades, scientists identified thirty-seven human carcinogens and over 500 substances that cause cancer in animals. Improved laboratory techniques also have made it possible to detect substances in miniscule amounts. Today, traces of substances can be found in foods in parts per billion, sometimes parts per trillion. This is equivalent to locating a few grains of sugar in an Olympic-size swimming pool.

The Delaney Dilemma

All of this has led to what is sometimes called the Delaney Dilemma. As Dr. W. Gary Flamm has stated:

> Given the extraordinarily low levels at which analytical chemists could measure chemical contaminants in food or anything else, all substances, no matter how pure, could be shown to be contaminated with one carcinogen or another.

And as a result,

> The idea that humans could be absolutely protected from chemical carcinogens died as a viable scientific concept.

An example of the dilemma came about when saccharin was shown conclusively to cause cancer in animals. The FDA removed it from the food supply. But Congress responded to strong demand from consumers, health professionals, and the food industry to pass legislation to allow saccharin to stay on the market provided it is labeled to warn that it is an animal carcinogen. This episode was of particular concern to people with diabetes, a disease that prevents them from using sugar in normal quantities in their diet. For these individuals, saccharin is an important sugar substitute in their foods.

Assessment of Risk

The FDA has attempted to balance the requirements of the Delaney Clause with the advances in food technology. Regulatory agencies of the United States government such as the FDA have developed a way of measuring the potential risk of harmful chemicals in foods. The method is called quantitative risk assessment (QRA) and has been under development since the early 1970s.

QRA is used by the regulatory agencies and by industry to assign a numerical value or score to the health risks of substances found in the environment, the workplace, or in foods or other products.

A QRA score is reached with four steps:

1. Determining whether a chemical is a health hazard.

2. Determining how much of the chemical produces an adverse health effect.

3. Determining the actual or anticipated human exposure over a certain period of time, such as an hour, a day, or a lifetime.

4. Calculating the size or magnitude of the risk—how many illnesses, birth defects, genetic

changes, deaths, or other harmful effects can be expected to result from a given exposure to the chemical.

The FDA uses the QRA to gauge the cancer-causing potential of chemical contaminants and animal drugs that may be detected in meat, fish, and poultry. For health risks other than cancer, the levels of exposure to food chemicals below which no harmful health effect will occur can be routinely measured. Then an extra safety margin 100 to 1000 times lower than the level at which no effect is seen is added.

The FDA has taken the position that a carcinogenic food chemical that presents no more than a one-in-one-million chance of causing cancer in a person's lifetime is "safe" for all practical purposes. In doing this, the FDA has invoked a *de minimis* doctrine. This is an established legal concept that says the law does not concern itself with trifles.

Total Diet Study

For twenty-nine years the FDA has conducted a program called the Total Diet Study. FDA investigators in twelve cities throughout the United States go grocery shopping four to five times a year and fill their carts with 234 selected food items.

The foods are sent to the FDA laboratory in Kansas City, Missouri, where chemists and technicians test each

Tea and coffee contain carcinogens which act as natural pesticides. Ceylon tea in this picture has a high quality reputation which is based on the careful plucking of only the top two leaves and curled leaf bud from each shoot of the tea bush.

item with equipment that can detect residues as small as one part per billion (ppb).

The Total Diet Study gauges pesticide residues that actually reach the table to be eaten. Traces of up to seventy or eighty pesticides have been detected in each market basket of food. However, these trace amounts are always within the safety limits set by the EPA and far below the acceptable daily intake (ADI) levels established by the United Nations' Food and Agriculture Organization and the World Health Organization.

$$\boxed{6}$$

How Are Pesticides Regulated in the United States?

For reasons of safety there is a need for the federal government to monitor and regulate pesticides. One case that illustrates this need occurred in 1986 in Van Buren, Arkansas.

The Need to Regulate Pesticides

The Food and Drug Administration's New Orleans laboratory discovered heptachlor, a synthetic pesticide similar to DDT, in seed and feed samples taken during an inspection of two companies in January and February of 1986. One of the companies had bought seed and grain to make a fuel called gasohol. Later, that company sold the leftover mash to another company, which then sold it to farmers in Arkansas, Missouri, and Oklahoma as animal feed.

The heptachlor-contaminated feed was produced in Van Buren, Arkansas, and found its way into the cows' milk as well as into products made from the milk of affected herds. The breast milk of nursing mothers who drank the contaminated cows' milk or ate products made from it was tainted with heptachlor.

Heptachlor presents a special risk in human breast milk. A mother's body absorbs the pesticide rapidly and stores it in fatty tissue for a year or more. The fat in breast milk may contain high levels of heptachlor. And a baby fed on heptachlor-contaminated breast milk may be found to have greater heptachlor levels than the mother.

In this case, the FDA had identified a serious problem. Heptachlor causes cancer in animals and may cause cancer in humans. The next question was, how widespread was the contamination?

FDA investigators and other scientists cooperated with local government officials to collect and test over 1,400 samples of milk and milk products produced within 150 miles of Van Buren. Contaminated milk and milk products were recalled from stores in Arkansas, Kansas, Louisiana, Missouri, Mississippi, Tennessee, Oklahoma, and Texas.

A U.S. attorney in Arkansas, on the recommendation of the FDA, forced the two companies involved to stop selling contaminated mash and feed. In addition,

The milk from dairy cattle can be contaminated with pesticides. The Food and Drug Administration (FDA) found heptachlor, a synthetic pesticide similar to DDT in milk in 1986. A mash contaminated with heptachlor mistakenly had been fed to dairy cattle.

federal, state, and local officials worked hard to protect people from the consequences of the contamination.

Suspect dairy herds were quarantined, and the states embargoed milk from the herds until tests showed it to be safe. Dairy products were held from market until analysis was completed.

The U.S. Department of Agriculture tested samples of meat to assure that any sold would be safe to eat. Investigators from the Centers for Disease Control in Atlanta, Georgia, collected blood and urine samples from families on farms where animals had been contaminated. The samples were checked for pesticide residues.

A joint task force from the FDA, USDA, and Environmental Protection Agency (EPA) visited farmers with quarantined herds and recommended that they receive assistance. The Farmer's Home Administration provided loans to the farmers who had lost their incomes due to the contamination. On July 2, 1987, President Ronald Reagan signed legislation passed by the U.S. Congress that provided eight million dollars to repay the farmers for their destroyed milk.

The University of Arkansas for Medical Science in Little Rock conducted free breast milk testing for almost 1,000 mothers who responded to its offer. Hundreds of other mothers had their milk checked by private laboratories. Most of the samples contained only low levels of heptachlor. Therefore, the risk for babies developing cancer from the milk was assessed to be very small.

As a result of this incident, heptachlor was banned for all uses in the United States in 1987.

FIFRA

The Federal Insecticide, Fungicide and Rodenticide Act (FIFRA) was enacted on June 25, 1947, and later amended as the Federal Pesticide Act of 1978. It regulates the distribution, sale, and use of pesticides in the United States. The Environmental Protection Agency (EPA) requires the registration or "formal listing with EPA of a new pesticide before it can be sold or distributed in intrastate or interstate commerce."

A pesticide licensed by the EPA must demonstrate that it "will not cause unreasonable adverse effects on human health or the environment when it is used according to approved label directions."

On October 25, 1988, President Reagan signed into law the FIFRA Amendments of 1988, which amended FIFRA to establish a five-phase program for the reregistration of pesticides. Pesticide producers must pay a registration maintenance fee to the EPA annually to reregister each pesticide they sell.

The pesticides given highest priority in the reregistration process include all pesticides for which registration standards have been issued. The remaining pesticides are placed into priority groups based upon several criteria: whether or not they are used on or in food or feed that may result in residues after harvest; may result in residues

71

that are toxic; are used in crops where worker exposure is likely to occur; or have significant outstanding requirements that make prompt review necessary.

The EPA has established the registration standards program as a way to review and reregister pesticides. The program describes EPA's evaluation of available data and the requirements that must be met by a pesticide producer to reregister its pesticide products.

The General Accounting Office estimated that the reregistering of pesticides might not be finished until 2024. For this reason, Congress passed amendments to set a new timetable for completing the review of pesticides by 1997. However, budget limitations may delay the completion of the review of pesticides until 2002.

President George Bush has presented a plan that would make it easier for the EPA to remove potentially hazardous pesticides from use. In addition, the plan would support ongoing reviews of data on safety and would toughen enforcement penalties. The plan would increase coordination among the federal agencies that regulate pesticides, and it also would replace the Delaney Clause with a negligible-risk standard.

7

Who Regulates What?

Food safety is the responsibility of local, state, national, and international government agencies. Within the United States, many agencies at various levels of government regulate and monitor the origin, composition, quality, safety, weight, labeling, packaging, marketing, and distribution of the food you eat and drink.

U.S. Regulatory Agencies

United States Department of Agriculture. The United States Department of Agriculture (USDA) inspects poultry, eggs, and domestic and imported meat and makes quality inspections to grade grains, fruits, vegetables, meat, poultry, eggs, and dairy products. Through its program of inspection and grading, it can enforce standards for wholesomeness and quality in these foods. The

USDA also does research in nutrition and works to educate the public about how to choose and cook foods for a healthy diet.

Environmental Protection Agency. The Environmental Protection Agency (EPA) regulates pesticides. It determines the safety of new pesticides and the tolerable levels of pesticide residues in foods and publishes safety directions for using pesticides. The EPA also sets water quality standards, which include the chemical content of water. Its guidelines are used to regulate bottled water sold for human drinking water in interstate commerce.

Food and Drug Administration. The Food and Drug Administration (FDA) is part of the Department of Health and Human Services' Public Health Service. This agency ensures the safety and wholesomeness of all foods sold in interstate commerce except for poultry, eggs, and meat, which are overseen by the USDA.

Standards for the composition, quality, nutrition, and safety of foods are set by the FDA. The FDA also does research to detect and prevent food contamination. It collects and interprets data on nutrition, on food additives, and on environmental factors that affect foods, such as pesticides. It is the FDA that enforces standards set by the EPA for pesticide residues.

The FDA also enforces federal regulations on food sanitation, labeling, food and color additives, and safety of foods. The FDA inspects food plants, imported foods, and feed mills that make feeds containing medications or nutritional supplements for animals that will be used for food for humans. And the FDA oversees recalls of contaminated or unsafe foods and has the authority to seize illegally marketed foods.

Department of Justice. The Department of Justice becomes involved when a problem food is in violation of federal law. Marshals from the Department of Justice have the authority to seize food products, and the Justice Department's attorneys can take suspected violators of food safety laws to court.

National Marine Fisheries Service. The National Marine Fisheries Service (NMFS) is a part of the Department of Commerce. It is responsible for seafood quality and identification, among other duties. The NMFS has a voluntary inspection program for fish products. It uses guidelines similar to the FDA regulations and that the FDA has authority to enforce.

States. States are responsible for inspecting restaurants, dairies, grain mills, and retail food businesses that are within their borders. States often can embargo illegal food products. Fishing waters within a state's jurisdiction are regulated by that state, and twenty-eight states have their own inspection programs to assure standards of quality for fish.

Federal agencies such as the FDA help states and local governments set uniform food safety standards and regulations and also assist them with guidelines, information, and research.

Dead fish in a stream are a familiar image of the results of pollution, agricultural runoff, and pesticide usage. The National Marine Fisheries Service (NMFS) is responsible for overseeing the quality of fish products.

Foreign Regulatory Agencies

The United States Food and Drug Administration, the Department of Agriculture, and the Environmental Protection Agency all work to insure the safety of foods imported into the United States. Nevertheless, the network of food protection these agencies provide cannot oversee all of the food products imported into the United States.

Codex Alimentarius. Consumers in the United States must also rely on foreign countries to produce foods that are safe to eat. An international organization, the Codex Alimentarius Commission, has an important role in maintaining and upgrading the quality of exporting countries' food products.

Codex Alimentarius was founded in 1962 by two United Nations organizations—the Food and Agricultural Organization (FAO) and the World Health Organization (WHO). Its purpose is to encourage fair international trade in food products and to promote the health and economic interests of consumers.

Codex Alimentarius has developed standards and codes for good manufacturing practices and technical specifications for food products and has set basic principles for trade in food products. For example, the Codex Code of Ethics for International Trade helps prevent the dumping of unsafe or inadequate quality foods in poorer countries by requiring countries to notify each other when they have refused entry of such food products.

Commodity standards for Codex are somewhat similar to the U.S. standards for the composition or identity of foods. To illustrate, the FDA requires that peanut butter be made from peanuts. And the USDA ensures that beef stew contains a specific percentage of beef. These may seem like obvious requirements, but imagine if you were severely allergic to walnuts and ate peanut butter that also contained ground walnuts as an unexpected ingredient. You could become very sick.

The Codex standards assure consumers in different countries that a food with the same name will:
- contain the same essential ingredients
- contain only the same approved food additives
- meet the same safety and quality specifications
- be weighed, measured, and tested in the same way
- be labeled in the same basic way

Codex Alimentarius has approximately 200 commodity standards to protect health and ease international trade in food products. To illustrate this, foods for special uses, including foods for infants and children, must meet Codex standards. This prevents toddler foods from being sold as substitutes for human breast milk, a practice that could endanger the health of infants.

In addition, Codex has over forty codes and guidelines for the production and processing of foods. For

United States grain being loaded on ships for export to foreign countries. Many of the food products exported and imported between countries are governed by international agreements, one of which is called Codex Alimentarius. Pesticides and food additives are two of the areas that Codex covers.

example, the Codex General Principles of Food Hygiene are used to train food workers worldwide. And codes of cleanliness and technological practice describe specifically how businesses should dehydrate fruits and vegetables, smoke fish, and quick-freeze vegetables.

Maximum levels are set by Codex for about 500 food additives. In July 1989, a commission meeting in Geneva, Switzerland, endorsed international use of certain additives to wheat flour that now are permitted in the United States.

Codex Alimentarius also has established about 2,700 maximum limits for pesticide residues in food and food crops. And several maximum residue limits for veterinary drugs are being considered for approval by Codex.

A Codex standard usually takes several years to be approved and accepted. A proposed draft standard goes through eight steps during which all member countries and committees review it. An independent scientific body of experts from around the world reviews the proposed draft standard for its scientific validity and soundness.

Next, committees of regulators must reach agreement on the practicality and enforceability of the standards or limits being proposed. If a country cannot develop its own standards for foods, it can adopt standards set by Codex with the assurance that the standards will be effective and allow them to successfully export their food products.

Codex Alimentarius is valuable because it provides a forum for the world's leading experts to discuss and reach sound scientific agreement on food safety issues that affect the international trade of food products. Also, some of the codes and standards adopted by Codex are modeled on the U.S. requirements. This means less testing is necessary by the FDA for imported foods that meet those Codex standards.

General Agreement on Tariffs and Trade. In addition to Codex Alimentarius, another organization has been working for more than forty years to maintain a legal framework for international trade. The United States and ninety-five other countries are members of the General Agreement on Tariffs and Trade (GATT).

Presently, a clause of GATT allows countries to adopt measures they deem necessary to protect human, animal, or plant life or health. The broad wording of this clause is viewed by the United States as a possible technical barrier to trade that may have nothing to do with health protection.

In April 1990, delegates at GATT talks agreed in principle to a reform that would require national health-related regulations to be consistent with scientific evidence. The delegates also agreed on an improved way of settling disputes that would rely on Codex and two other international scientific organizations.

One of these organizations is the International Office of Epizootics (IOE), which concerns itself with the health and sanitary requirements for the import and export of animals. The other organization is the International Plant Protection Conference (IPPC), which oversees plant quarantine requirements to prevent the international spread of plant diseases and pests.

Food and Agricultural Organization. The twenty-third conference of the FAO was held in Rome, Italy, in November, 1985. The 158-nation conference is the FAO's supreme governing body. Ministers from 110 countries approved an international code of conduct on the distribution and use of pesticides, which is the first set of international guidelines for the handling, trade, and safe use of pesticides. It will be particularly useful to developing countries that lack controls over the use of pesticides.

8

Ways to Reduce Pesticide Use Now

Many methods currently are available to farmers to help them reduce the use of pesticides on their crops. Some of the techniques are traditional, time-honored ways to cope with crop pests, while others are new and innovative. Growers are learning to combine both the old and new methods to better manage their farms and to minimize the quantities of pesticides that they apply to their crops.

Traditional Nonchemical Techniques

Plowing. Plowing under the remains of a harvested crop reduces some insect pests by preventing the hatching of eggs or pupae that were laid on or attached to the plants. In addition, burying the remains of fungus-infected crop plants helps prevent the spread of diseases.

Plowing fields with pre-World War II plows. Today, farmers are trying to reduce the use of pesticides by combining new and innovative methods with the traditional, time-honored ways.

Tilling the soil at a particular time in the life cycle of a pest can greatly reduce the number of pests that survive. For example, deep plowing in the spring to bury all leftover corn plants destroys many of the larvae of the European corn borer. And the wheat stem sawfly can be reduced by as much as 75 percent by turning under wheat stubble after a harvest.

The timing of when a crop is harvested can also be important to keeping pests under control. If sweet potatoes are harvested as soon as they are ready, damage by the sweet potato weevil is kept at a minimum. The same is true for Irish potatoes and the potato tuberworm, as well as for peas and the pea weevil.

The removal of the seeds produced by weeds is a time-tested way of getting rid of these types of pests. An example is sorting out dodder seeds from a mixture of crop seeds, such as clover. Dodder is a weed that draws some of its nourishment from the crop plants, thus weakening the crop plants and reducing the yield.

Crop Rotation. Another method to help keep pests in check is crop rotation. A crop planted in a particular field one year is replaced by another unrelated crop in the next planting. The pests that attack the first crop are unable to feed on the next crop. For example, white-fringed beetles reproduce well on peanuts and soybeans. If the next crop planted in the same fields is a grain plant such as corn, the adult beetles lay few eggs, and the population of this insect pest is kept at tolerable levels.

Sometimes the spread of disease can be prevented by quarantining. Infected crops are not allowed to go to another region or country. Because quarantines disrupt trade between countries, exporting countries have authorities that can certify their crops as being disease-free. This usually means that a crop has been thoroughly inspected for disease before being offered for export.

Disease sometimes can be controlled or eliminated by destroying infected plants. Citrus canker was introduced to the United States from Japan in 1911. To get rid of it, over four million orange, grapefruit, and lemon trees in Florida groves were destroyed at a cost of millions of dollars. It took until 1927 before the disease was completely cleared from Florida. Additional trees had to be destroyed in other states as well before the disease was defeated.

Biological Controls. Biological control of pests uses the natural enemies of pests to keep their population in check. The idea is very old. Natural insect enemies of pests were used in ancient China. The Chinese raised a particular species of ant (*Oecophylla smaragdina*) in their mandarin orange trees to control caterpillars and large boring beetles. The ants built large paperlike nests in the citrus trees that contained thousands of individuals. The Chinese helped the ants move between trees by placing bamboo runways from one tree to another and would even buy and sell the nests.

A famous U.S. example of the control of a pest

through use of a natural enemy is the case of a tiny insect pest known as the cottony cushion scale (*Icerya purchasi* Maskell). By the late 1860s, the citrus crop had become a thriving, important industry in California. About 1868 the cottony cushion scale was introduced into the United States, probably on lemon trees imported from Australia. In just a few years, the branches of trees in California citrus groves were covered with snowlike masses containing thousands of the eggs of this insect. The citrus crop was being devastated.

Alarmed citrus growers appealed to their representatives in Congress and to Charles Riley, chief of the United States Department of Agriculture's division of entomology. Riley's assistant, Albert Koebele, eventually went to Australia where he discovered a natural enemy of cottony cushion scale. It was a black and red lady beetle called the vedalia beetle (*Vedalia cardinalis*). He collected some of the beetles and sent them back to California where they were introduced to fight the insect.

The vedalia beetle wiped out the cottony cushion scale within two years and saved the California citrus orchards. This case established biological control as a valid method all over the world.

Another example of biological control of a pest by a natural insect enemy is that of the green lacewing (*Chrysopa carnea*) against the cotton boll weevil (*Anthonomus grandis*). Cotton is a major fiber crop in the southern states of the United States as well as in other countries.

In one experiment, green lacewings reduced the larvae of the boll weevil by 96 percent on cotton crops in Texas.

Other helpful insects destroy a wide variety of harmful insects. For instance, Tachinid flies, which look like large houseflies, prey upon insects that eat crops, such as European earwigs, gypsy moths, Japanese beetles, tomato hornworms, brown-tail moths, and grasshoppers. Syrphid flies prey upon aphids and also help pollinate crops.

One species of wasp with the name *Trichogramma* destroys the eggs of many harmful moths and butterflies. *Trichograma* wasps also have been used with success to protect cotton crops. In Mexico, the government established insectaries scattered throughout the country to raise these wasps for control of the boll weevil.

Fungi, Bacteria, and Viruses Can Control Pests

Some fungi attack eelworms and are known as predacious fungi. The potato eelworm forms cysts, each of which contains from fifty to six hundred eggs. The cysts are highly chemical-resistant. A cyst may survive for years in the soil only to hatch when it comes into contact with juices produced by the roots of the potato plant. In England and in other countries, the discovery of predacious fungi that control these eelworms has helped solve the problem.

Another fungus that can be used against nematode roundworm garden pests is *Arthrobotrys*. This fungus produces tiny round knobs coated with a sticky substance that kills the small round worms when they come into contact with it. The knobs sometimes are called "lethal lollipops."

Microbial pesticides are bacteria, viruses, or chemicals that are commercially produced and can be used to attack and destroy pests. One example is the control of Japanese beetles by a milky spore disease caused by the bacterium *Bacillus popilliae*. After a bacterial dust of *B. popilliae* was spread over crops, Japanese beetles no longer ravaged field crops, fruits, or vegetables in Eastern states from New Hampshire to North Carolina and all the way west to Ohio.

Milky spore disease is spread by infected beetle grubs. When the worm-like larvae die, bacteria that have multiplied in their bodies are released into the soil and infect other, healthy, grubs. In addition, *B. popilliae* produces spores that can remain alive in the soil for many years.

In 1927 a bacterium with the scientific name *Bacillus thuringiensis* was noted as a natural enemy of many insect pests. The bacterium produces a toxic chemical that kills insects. It is commercially produced and used mainly to control moth pests. *B. thuringiensis* also produces a substance called fly toxin that interferes with the growth of houseflies.

Viruses also have shown promise as a way to control insect pests. A virus called *polyhedrosis* produces disease in the cabbage looper, a serious insect pest. As long as the temperature is 21°C (70°F) or above, this virus will kill the cabbage looper within four or five days. For several days after they hatch, young cabbage looper caterpillars feed on the lower leaves on the cabbage plant, so it is only necessary to apply the virus to these lower leaves. In this way, the head of cabbage that goes to market remains untouched.

Viral diseases have been found that appear capable of controlling several insect pests, including spider mites, the alfalfa caterpillar, and the red-banded leaf roller, a major moth pest of apple trees in the Northeast.

Integrated Pest Management

Reducing the use of synthetic pesticides is the goal of an ecologically-based approach to pest control called integrated pest management (IPM). With this method several different techniques are combined to maintain pests below damaging levels. The practice of IPM protects the environment, maintains food quality, and allows farmers to remain competitive in the marketplace.

The integrated pest management program for individual crops may be somewhat different, but all IPM programs have certain similarities.

One important component of IPM is the regular monitoring of crops. Scouts go into the crop-growing fields or orchards and count the population of pests as well as that of their natural enemies. The potential damage to a crop can be determined from the data collected by the scouts on pest levels and natural enemy levels, as well as the growth stage of the crop, and the weather.

With the data collected by scouts, informed decisions can be made on whether it is necessary to apply a pesticide, which kind to use, and the minimal amount needed to protect the crop from significant damage.

With IPM, actions to control pests are taken only when a threshold is reached. This occurs when the numbers of pests reach levels that will cause sufficient damage to justify action.

Integrated pest management employs cultural practices, soil testing, sanitation, use of resistant varieties, use of biological controls, and use of pesticides. Cultural practices reduce pest populations by making their environment less favorable. These include modifying planting, cultivation, growing, and harvesting practices to reduce pest damage.

Soil testing insures that the crop is grown under the best possible conditions. Sanitation removes sources of pest infestation by ridding fields or orchards of crop refuse, sterilizing transplants, and destroying plants that may harbor pests.

The planting of resistant varieties of crops results in less pesticide required than in more susceptible varieties. The resistant varieties are better able to avoid, tolerate, or recover from pest injuries.

Whenever possible, integrated pest management uses natural enemies to control pests. These natural enemies include predators, parasites, and diseases. In integrated pest management, natural enemies may be introduced to control pests, or if already present, they may be encouraged by providing a suitable habitat for them. Choosing the proper pesticide and timing its application so as not to harm these natural enemies also helps.

When pesticides are used in an integrated pest management program, they are selected carefully to cause the least environmental disruption and the lowest toxicity for beneficial species as well as for humans. In addition, the amount of pesticide applied is the lowest effective amount that can be used.

IPM in an Apple Orchard

From the 1950s into the 1970s, apple growers used calendar-based programs to determine when they sprayed pesticides onto their orchards. Typically, spraying was done every ten days. But now apple growers understand that pesticides must be applied in minimal amounts and with great care. They are aware of increasing costs, the development of pesticide resistance by several fruit pests, and the demands of the public to reduce pesticides in the environment.

There are many apple pests, including insects, mites, various diseases, and animals such as meadow voles and deer. One of the best known insect apple pests is the codling moth, *Laspeyresia pomonella.*

An adult codling moth is about one-half inch long. A larva (the infamous "worm" in the apple!) burrows into the developing fruit and eats the seeds. The larva grows to about three-quarters of an inch long at maturity and then crawls out of the damaged fruit and drops to the ground. Some larvae go into hibernation to overwinter, and others pupate and produce a second generation of adults that can attack the next season's apples.

Apple growers can monitor the codling moth population using a pheromone trap placed in the center of a ten to fifteen acre section of a commerical orchard when the trees bloom. Pheromones are highly potent chemical scents produced by insects to attract their own kind. Chemists have been able to imitate pheromones to attract and trap specific species of insect pests. Codling moth traps are inspected daily until the first males are captured and then twice a week. Captured moths are recorded and removed from the trap.

From about three weeks after the apple blossom petals drop until harvest, growers examine ten apples from one apple tree on each three to five acres of orchard to see if there is any damage from codling moth larvae. In addition, temperature data are collected every week from monitoring stations in the orchard.

Research at Michigan State University has led to a predictive model of codling moth development. From this model and the information derived from the monitoring, it is possible to predict critical points in the codling moth life cycle. Newly emerged larvae are highly susceptible to insecticide sprays. If insecticide is applied after the first egg hatches and before 50 percent of the eggs hatch, it will have the maximum effect in disrupting codling moth development.

Apple scab (*Venturis inaequalis*) is an important disease. It is caused by a fungus that produces olive-colored blotches on the undersides of leaves and circular scabs on the fruit. Fruit that has been damaged cannot be sold for as high a price as scab-free fruit, so the disease is economically important to apple growers.

The fungus overwinters in dead, fallen leaves. During wet periods in the spring, spores are released that can infect the leaves and fruit of apple trees. The release of spores is believed to occur during the first thirty minutes of a rain. But if rain lasts for two or three days, additional spores are released.

Researchers have learned that a film of water must be present on the surface of the leaves and fruit for a certain period of time in order for infection to occur. The length of the period during which infection can occur depends upon the temperature. Researchers have named the relationship between wetness periods, temperature, and apple scab infection Mills' infection period.

A modified hygrothermograph placed in the orchard measures how long leaves and fruit are wet as well as

The codling moth is a well known pest to apples. Apple growers are trying to minimize pesticide usage by using integrated pest management techniques. Growers can determine the precise day to spray pesticides to kill the codling moth, thereby reducing the need to spray more often.

temperature and humidity. This instrument records data the grower can compare to a chart showing Mills' infection period. Following this chart, the grower can see that it must rain for more than two days for infection to occur when the temperature is less than 5°C (41°F), whereas at 10°C (50°F) leaves and fruit must be wet for a minimum of fourteen hours for apple scab infection to occur.

Further research has revealed that the apple scab fungus can tell the difference between night and day! The fungus does not release spores at night, so apple growers now know that they do not need to worry about apple scab infection when it rains at night.

Several apple scab fungus resistant varieties of apples have been developed that eventually may make the use of fungicides to control apple scab disease practically unnecessary. Among these are apples with names such as Jonafree, Freedom, and Liberty. The Liberty apple, which became available about the mid-1980s, may be a winner. It has shown resistance to rust, mildew, and fire blight as well.

Mites on apple trees are frequent pests. Three varieties of mites affect apples in New Hampshire: the European red mite, the two-spotted spider mite, and the apple rust mite. However, growers are being taught to preserve another mite (*Amblyseius fallacis* Garman) because it preys upon the mites that are pests. Researchers also have learned that some pesticides should be avoided to encourage *A. fallacis* as a natural enemy of harmful

Apple Scab: Temperature—Wet Period Guide

Average Temperature* (°F)	Hours of Wet Foliage Necessary for Leaf Infection
78	13
77	11
76	9½
61 to 75	9
60	9½
57 to 59	10
55 to 56	11
54	11½
52 to 53	12
51	13
50	14
49	14½
48	15
47	17
46	19
45	20
44	22
43	25
42	30
33 to 41	More than 2 days
* Average temperature during wetting period should be determined from hourly readings.	

Source: *1990 New England Apple Spray Guide,* Cooperative Extension Service, Universities of Connecticut, Maine, Massachusetts, New Hampshire, Rhode Island, and Vermont, p. 4.

mites. *A. fallacis* now is available commercially for growers to use in their orchards.

The goal of IPM is to provide growers with high yields of top-quality fruit while at the same time reducing pesticide use. By combining biological, cultural, and chemical control methods, IPM helps growers achieve these goals.

Growers who practice IPM have an intimate knowledge of the numbers and kinds of pests in their orchards and the natural enemies that are present. They scout and monitor their orchards to decide if a pesticide application is necessary, the minimum effective amount to use, and when to apply it for maximum results.

In many orchards where IPM programs are being practiced, the quantities of pesticides being used today are only about half the amounts used fifteen years ago.

Study Confirms the Possibility of Reducing Pesticide Usage

Programs that incorporate many of the principles of IPM are being tried on major crops. A recent study was conducted by scientists at Cornell University on forty major food crops. It showed that pesticide use in the United States could be reduced by up to 50 percent without reducing crop yields by using methods such as those adopted for IPM programs.

In addition, the Cornell study emphasizes the greater use of scouting to determine pest and natural enemy levels. It also encourages the use of improved pesticide application equipment and treat-only-when-necessary programs to reduce the quantities of pesticides being applied, and it mentions the innovative use of vacuuming machines that are capable of sucking insect pests off crops such as soybeans.

A California-based company, Tanimura and Antle, has developed a fleet of forty-eight vacuum machines that suck up insects from lettuce crops it grows in California, Arizona, and Mexico. These giant vacuum cleaners are called "Salad Vacs" and are 85 percent effective against flying insects. Vacuum cleaners also can be used effectively on strawberry and soybean crops.

In the Cornell study, scouting methods used along with forecasting were able to reduce the use of fungicides on tomatoes grown in Pennsylvania by 55 percent.

Improved pesticide application equipment and methods could reduce the amount of pesticide wasted by misapplication by 50 percent or more. For example, the study points out that only 25 to 50 percent of pesticide applied to a crop by aircraft actually reaches the targeted crop. Ground sprayers increase the amount of pesticide reaching the target to 75 percent. In addition, a ground sprayer can be outfitted with a shroud to prevent drifting pesticide spray into the surrounding environment. Methods other than spraying can be used on some crops such as cotton and soybeans.

Among other agricultural alternatives to pesticides that the Cornell researchers identified are:

- Plant crops in a denser pattern to crowd out weeds
- Mow weeds instead of applying herbicides
- Use biological controls to take advantage of the natural enemies of pests
- Use field scouting to determine when pesticides are needed rather than following a routine calendar application
- Use methods of applying pesticides that are less wasteful, such as recirculating sprayers, shrouded sprayers that prevent drifting pesticide spray, and ground-application equipment
- Use improved plant varieties that have natural pest resistance or that grow in a short season and thus avoid some pests
- Use insect traps that lure and capture insects with pheromones
- Use vacuum machines to remove insects from crops
- Use crop rotation to discourage the buildup of insects, weeds, and diseases that attack specific crops

Benefits of Reducing Pesticide Usage

Some of the methods cited to reduce pesticide usage may increase certain costs to farmers. However, some of their expenses to purchase and apply pesticides may be decreased. In addition, reduced costs for the monitoring of pesticide residues in our food supplies,

The "Salad Vac" vacuums insects off lettuce crops in the field. A California company uses forty-eight vacuum machines to suck up insects from its crops. They can also be used effectively on strawberry and soybean crops.

groundwater, and the environment by agencies such as the EPA, FDA, and USDA would benefit all consumers.

More importantly, the reduction of pesticide usage will promote long-term well-being for everyone. Decreasing the amounts of pesticides used on food crops will insure that the U.S. food supply remains ". . . the safest in the world," as Fred Shank, director of the FDA's Center for Food Safety and Applied Nutrition has said. It also will help restore public confidence in the safety of their food supply.

In addition, curtailing pesticide usage will further protect wildlife and their natural habitat.

Conclusion

During the 1940s synthetic pesticides became available. At first they appeared to be a boon in the struggles to provide enough food for a hungry world and to rid people of pests that carry deadly diseases.

By the 1950s, however, doubts arose about the safety of these new pesticides, including DDT, a pesticide that had saved over one million human lives from typhus and plague epidemics during World War II but was found to be accumulating in the environment, killing countless birds and other wildlife. People became aware of and shared a growing concern about the safety of the presence of a variety of synthetic pesticides in their food supply, in groundwater, and throughout the environment.

Because people fear damage to the Earth's environment and natural resources more than nuclear war or an arms race, they have voiced their concerns about the unwise or excessive use of pesticides. Studies done by researchers at Cornell University indicate that it is possible to reduce pesticide use by up to 50 percent on some crops without affecting yields.

Cornell researchers concluded that:

> The 50 percent pesticide reduction . . . would help satisfy the concerns of the majority of the public, who worry about pesticide levels in their food and damage to the environment. . . . In addition, it is clear that the public would accept some reduction in cosmetic standards if this would result in a decrease in pesticide contamination of food.

More and more growers are rediscovering traditional nonchemical methods of pest control such as crop rotation. They also are adopting newer techniques, such as integrated pest management, that require a dynamic, intimate knowledge of the lives of crop pests and their natural enemies. These methods of pest control allow for the cautious, careful use of pesticides on an only-when-necessary basis.

Growers using heedful, conscientious approaches to farming incorporate an array of solutions to pest management that remind us of "the other road" so eloquently set forth in 1962 by Rachel Carson in *Silent Spring.* Today, sense about safety means avoiding the use of synthetic pesticides whenever alternatives are possible. And when pesticides must be used, sense about safety means selecting those that are least harmful and using them "thoughtfully, with full awareness that what we do may have consequences remote in time and place."

List of Abbreviations

ADI—acceptable daily intake
ANTU—alpha-napthylthiourea
CWA—Clean Water Act
DDT—dichloro-diphenyl-trichloroethane
EBDC—ethylenebisdithiocarbamate
EDB—ethylene dibromide
EPA—Environmental Protection Agency
ETU—ethylenethiourea
FAO—Food and Agricultural Organization
FDA—Food and Drug Administration
FIFRA—Federal Insecticide, Fungicide and Rodenticide Act
GATT—General Agreement on Tariffs and Trade
HA—health advisory
IOE—International Office of Epizootics
IPM—integrated pest management
IPPC—International Plant Protection Conference
MCL—maximum contaminant level
NMFS—National Marine Fisheries Service
NRDC—National Resources Defense Council
ppb—parts per billion
ppt—parts per trillion
QRA—quantitative risk assessment
TCDD—2,3,7,8-tetrachloro-dibenzo-p-dioxin
UMDH—unsymmetrical dimethylhydrazine
USDA—U.S. Department of Agriculture
WHO—World Health Organization

Chapter References

Chapter 1

Borror, Donald J., and Dwight M. Delong. *An Introduction to the Study of Insects.* New York: Rinehart & Co. 1954, pp. 836–838.

Fletcher, W. W. *The Pest War.* New York: John Wiley & Sons (© Basil Blackwell), 1974, pp. 6, 7, 10, 11, 17.

Pringle, Laurence. *Pests and People.* New York: Macmillan, 1972, ch. 3.

USA Today, December 1988, p. 3.

Villee, Claude A. *Biology.* Philadelphia: Saunders, 1967, pp. 152, 175–177.

Zim, Herbert S., and Clarence Cottam. *Insects: A Guide to Familiar American Insects.* New York: Golden Press, 1956, pp. 11, 94, 100.

Chapter 2

"Antibiotics in Animal Feed." *Nightline* transcript, ABC-TV, January 25, 1985.

Ballentine, C. "Deep Trouble." *FDA Consumer,* September 1981, pp. 31–34.

Bonfante, J. "Medfly Madness." *Time,* January 8, 1990, p. 51.

Campt, D. "A Look at the Basics: Reducing Dietary Risk." *EPA Journal,* May/June 1990, p. 20.

Carson, Rachel. *Silent Spring.* Boston: Houghton Mifflin, 1962, pp. x, 15, 16, 27, 28, 30, 83–85, 155, 256, 257.

"Chlordane Sales Halted." *Science News,* August 15, 1987, p. 102.

Fletcher, W. W. *The Pest War.* New York: John Wiley & Sons (© Basil Blackwell), 1974, p. 48, 49, 82–84, 195.

MacKenzie, D.. "Call to Unleash Dieldrin on Locust Plague." *New Scientist,* September 15, 1988, pp. 26–27.

———— "Locust Plague Threatens North Africa." *New Scientist,* March 31, 1988, p. 17.

Melanby, K. "With Safeguards, DDT Should Still be Used." *The Wall Street Journal,* September 12, 1989, p. A26.

1990 Farm Chemicals Handbook. Willoughby, Ohio: Meister, 1990, pp. 8, 13, 36, 53, 65.

Pimental, David, et al. "Environmental and Economic Impacts of Reducing U.S. Agricultural Pesticide Use." In *Handbook on Pest*

Management in Agriculture. Boca Raton, Fla.: CRC Press, 1991, pp. 679–681.

Schmidt, W. E. "In the Great Lakes, Some Pollution Defies the Cleanup." *The New York Times,* July 2, 1989, p. E5.

Segal, M. "EBDCs Becoming a Household Word." *FDA Consumer,* March 1990, p. 15.

Whitten, Jamie L. *That We May Live.* Princeton, N.J.: Van Nostrand, 1966, p. 51.

Chapter 3

"Agriculture in Transition." *Issues in Science and Technology,* Fall 1985, pp. 99–102, 103, 107.

Brown, Lester R. "The Grain Drain." *The Futurist,* July–August 1989, pp. 9–11, 13.

Campt, D. "A Look at the Basics: Reducing Dietary Risks," graph on U.S. agricultural pesticide usage in 1988, *EPA Journal,,* May/June 1990, p. 20.

Heer, David M. *Society and Population.* Englewood Cliffs, N.J.: Prentice-Hall, 1968, pp. 3, 4.

Metcalf, M., and W. Luckmann. *Introduction to Insect Pest Management.* New York: John Wiley and Sons, 1975, p. 236.

Pimental, David, et al. "Environmental and Economic Impacts of Reducing U.S. Agricultural Pesticide Use." Boca Raton, Fla.: CRC Press, 1991, p. 680, 681.

Whitten, Jamie L. *That We May Live.* Princeton, N.J.: Van Nostrand, 1966, pp. 7–9.

Chapter 4

"Agriculture in Transition." *Issues in Science and Technology,* Fall 1985, pp. 134, 135, 137–140.

Groundwater Questions/Answers, rev. ed., Wilmington, Del.: Dupont Chemical Co., November 1988, pp. 1, 2, 4.

Nash, J. Madeleine, "It's Ugly, But It Works." *Time,* May 21, 1990, p. 29.

Pimentel, David, et al. "Environmental and Economic Impacts of Reducing U.S. Agricultural Pesticide Use." In *Handbook on Pest Management in Agriculture.* Boca Raton, Fla.: CRC Press, 1991, p. 680.

Chapter 5

"A is for Apple." *60 Minutes* transcript, CBS-TV, February 26, 1989, pp. 11, 13.

"Alar Withdrawn From U.S. Market." *Boston Globe*, June 3, 1989, p. 3.

Benson, J. S. "Facing a Tough Issue: An FDA View." *EPA Journal*, May/June 1990, p. 10, 11.

Bidinotto, R. J. "The Great Apple Scare." *Reader's Digest*, large-type ed., October 1990, pp. 23–25.

"Does Everything Cause Cancer?" *Consumers' Research*, May 1989, pp. 11, 12, 14, 15.

Flieger, K. "The Delaney Dilemma." *FDA Consumer* Special Report, Safety First: Protecting America's Food Supply, November 1988, p. 37.

———. "How Safe is Safe?" *FDA Consumer*, September 1988, pp. 16, 17.

Garland, Anne Witte. *For Our Kids' Sake*. San Francisco: Sierra Club Books, 1989, sec. 3.

Henry, S. "An Apple a Day." *Technology Review*, February/March 1988, p. 11.

MacKerron, C. "Dioxin and Milk Don't Mix." *Chemical Week*, September 20, 1989, p. 15.

"Pesticides: The Circle of Poison." *Nightline* transcript, ABC-TV June 1, 1989, pp. 3, 4.

Raloff, Janet. "Dioxin: Is Everyone Contaminated?" *Science News*, July 13, 1985, p. 26, 29.

Residues in Foods—1988. FDA Pesticide Program, p. 8.

Russell, C. "A Crisis in Public Confidence." *EPA Journal*, May/June 1990, p. 2.

"Safety First: Protecting America's Food Supply—Part Three." *FDA Consumer*, October 1988, p. 1.

Segal, M. "EDBCs Becoming a Household Word." *FDA Consumer*, March 1990, pp. 14–16.

"What About Apples?" *60 Minutes* transcript, CBS-TV, May 14, 1989, pp. 3, 5, 6.

Chapter 6

Farley, D. "Investigators' Reports: From Tainted Feed to Mother's Milk." *FDA Consumer*, March 1987, pp. 38–40.

1990 Farm Chemicals Handbook. Willoughby, Ohio.: Meister, 1990, pp. D2, D3, D8–D10.

Russell, C. "A Crisis in Public Confidence." *EPA Journal*, May/June 1990, p. 5.

Chapter 7

"Safety First: Protecting America's Food Supply." *FDA Consumer,* July/August 1988, p. 18.

"Twenty-third Conference of the FAO Adopts Pesticide Code, Food Security Compact." *UN Chronicle,* January 1986, p. 61.

Chapter 8

Carson, Rachel. *Silent Spring.* Boston: Houghton Mifflin, 1962, p. 278.

DeBach, Paul. *Biological Control by Natural Enemies.* London: Cambridge University Press, 1974, pp. 71, 92, 97, 221, 223–225, 257, 260.

Eaton, Alan T. *Mites on Apple Trees.* Cooperative Extension Service, Fact Sheet 7. Durham, N.H.: University of New Hampshire, 1985.

Fletcher, W. W. *The Pest War.* New York: John Wiley & Sons (© Basil Blackwell), 1974, pp. 22, 23, 27–29, 32, 115, 124, 125.

Hollingsworth, C. S. and W. M. Coli. *Integrated Pest Management: What is IPM?* Cooperative Extension Service Bulletin. Amherst, Mass.: University of Massachusetts, May 1989.

Hunter, Beatrice Trum. *Gardening Without Poisons.* Boston: Houghton Mifflin, 1971, pp. 23, 24, 42, 43, 187, 188, 193, 197.

Integrated Management of Apple Pests. Cooperative Extension Service, Bulletin C-169. Amherst, Mass.: University of Massachusetts, 1984.

1990 New England Apple Spray Guide. Cooperative Extension Service, Universities of Connecticut, Maine, Massachusetts, New Hampshire, Rhode Island, and Vermont. p. 4, 5.

Pimentel, David, et al. "Environmental and Economic Impacts of Reducing U.S. Agricultural Pesticide Use." In *Handbook on Pest Management in Agriculture.* Boca Raton, Fla.: CRC Press, 1991, pp. 686, 679, 703.

Pringle, Laurence. *Pests and People.* New York: Macmillan, 1972, p. 55.

Russell, C. "A Crisis in Public Confidence." *EPA Journal,* May/June 1990, p. 2.

Index

P

parathion, 24
pea weevil, 85
pentachlorophenol, 58
People's Republic of
    China, 33
pesticide, 7, 18
pheromones, 93
plague, 19, 29, 102
plowing, 83, 84
pollution, 38, 43
polyhedrosis, 89
polyvinyl chloride, 58
Population Institute, 35
potato blight, 12, 26
potato cyst eelworm, 11, 88
potato tuberworm, 85
powdery mildew, 26
predacious fungi, 88
Public Health Service, 74

Q

quantitative risk assessment
    (QRA), 63, 64
quarantining, 86

R

Reagan, President Ronald,
    70
red-banded leaf roller, 90
reregister pesticides, 71, 72
residues, 40, 47, 51, 59,
    66, 71
resistance, 21, 91, 96
Riley, Charles, 87
Rocky Mountain spotted
    fever, 11
rodenticide, 18, 28, 29
rootworm, 45

S

saccharin, 62, 63
Safe Drinking Water Act,
    45

Safe Drinking Water Act
    (1974 and 1980), 45
Salad Vac, 99, 101
Sandlin, Jay, 53
Schecter, Arnold, 55
Science, 50
Sencor (metrabuzin), 44
Shank, Fred, 102
Silent Spring, 21, 22, 24,
    103
60 Minutes (CBS News
    program), 48, 53
soil erosion, 38, 40
Soviet Union, 33
State University of New
    York in Binghamton,
    55
Swedish EPA, 58
sweet potato weevil, 85
syrphid flies, 88

T

Tachinid flies, 88
Tanimura and Antle, 99
TCDD
    (2,3,7,8-tetrachloro-dib
    enzo-p-dioxin), 55
1080 (sodium
    fluoroacetate), 29
terbacil, 28
Texas fever, 11
ticks, 11
tomato hornworms, 88
Total Diet Study, 64, 66
Trichogramma wasps, 88
tularemia, 11
typhus, 19, 29, 102

U

U.S. Centers for Disease
    Control, 70
UDMH (unsymmetrical
    dimethylhydrazine),
    48, 51, 53

Uniroyal Chemical
    Company, 54
United Nations Food and
    Agriculture
    Organization (FAO),
    20, 33, 66, 77
United Nations World
    Food Council, 35
United States Census
    Bureau, 37
United States Department
    of Agriculture
    (USDA), 8, 53, 70,
    73, 77, 87
University of Arkansas for
    Medical Science, 70
University of Bordeaux, 25
University of Iowa, 44

V

vedalia beetle (*Vedalia
    cardinalis*), 87
viruses, 15

W

warfarin, 28
wheat stem sawfly, 85
white-fringed beetles, 85
World Bank, 36
World Future Society, 7
World Health
    Organization
    (WHO), 66, 77
world population, 30, 34
World War II, 18, 19, 26,
    84

Z

Zeidler, Othmar, 18